The Feed Your Spirit Series

Forty Days Spirit Led

Devotions

REV. RAPHAEL CHRISTOPHER

Published by TESTAMARK BOOKS

Testamarkbooks@hotmail.com

Feed Your Spirit Devotionals Series

Copyright 2017 © Rev. Raphael Christopher

Published in the United Kingdom by Testamark Books

Issued: June 2017

Paperback: ISBN 978-1-9997591-0-0

Ebook: ISBN 978 – 9-1-9997591-1-7

Email the author or Testamark Books at
testamarkbooks@hotmail.com

Printed by Biddles Books, King's Lynn, Norfolk PE32 1SF

Dedications and Acknowledgements

This book is dedicated to The Almighty God, The Lord Jesus and The Holy Spirit who has counted me faithful and appointed me to serve him and the body of Christ; and to my late parents, Chief Christopher & 'Amazing' Grace Osili; my wife Jo; my daughter Chloe; all Living Word Bible Church members; Amakom and Osili family members; the Burcham, Reynolds family members; Rev. Wendy Preston & James Preston; Rev. Terry & Mersa Wares; Rev. R.T & Louise Kendall; Bishop Joe & Laura Corry; friends; enemies and others too numerous to count, who taught me through their actions; examples; Christian faith; love and encouragement to serve God and the body of Christ by Love through the Word of God no matter what.

Introduction

In Matthew 4:4 and Luke 4:4 we see it written that Jesus answered Satan and said

"...It is written: 'Man shall not live on bread alone, but on every word that comes from the mouth of God...'"

I want you to notice in the biblical record of the book of Luke, that our Lord Jesus for the past forty days of his temptation in the desert, did not eat any food (**notice it does not say that Jesus did not drink anything for those forty days**) and we learn that for that forty days, He was tempted by the devil.

We often hear it being said that Jesus was only tempted after the end of the forty days but this view is not backed by scripture as you see in the above account in the gospel of Luke. The correct view, I believe should be that Jesus was tempted continuously by the Devil for those forty days otherwise it makes no sense for Jesus to only fast for the forty days and then only have three temptations at the end of it.

Now, we know that when the forty days had ended, Jesus was hungry...and the Devil tempted Jesus to turn stone into bread and eat.

This reply of Jesus is the reason for the feed your spirit book series. The 40 days of fasting is the reason for the title of this book in the series – 40 days devotions.

Jesus is telling us that we cannot live by physical food alone. We also have to live by spiritual food. We know from 1 Thessalonians 5:23 that we have a spirit and soul and body and since the word of God is spirit according to John 6:63 so when you feed on the word of God, you are feeding your spirit and your spirit become strong and a blessing to you and your community in the name of Jesus.

Moreover, God told Joshua in Joshua 1:8 to keep the words of God in his heart and do them and then he will have success and prosperity. And we know that Joshua did obey and The Lord made him to succeed and prosper.

Since we know God is no respecter of persons according to Acts 10:34, God will do the same for you! So let's begin this exciting 40 days adventure & supernatural walk with God.

Contents

DAY 1

Scripture KJV: Psalm 51:1

"... {To the chief Musician, A Psalm of David, when Nathan the prophet came unto him, after he had gone in to Bathsheba.} Have mercy upon me, O God, according to thy lovingkindness..."

Commentary:

One of the most important everlasting attributes of our Heavenly Father is his Mercy. *2 Cor 1:13* tells us that God is the Father of Mercies. In fact, his Throne is described as The 'Mercy Seat' according to Smith's Bible Dictionary. *Exodus 25:17* describes the Mercy Seat of the Ark of the Covenant in the Tabernacle. *Hebrews 8:5* tells us that the earthly tabernacle is a copy of the Heavenly Tabernacle. This means there is an everlasting Heavenly Tabernacle containing The Mercy Seat. At the Mercy Seat, we receive mercy and the word 'Mercies' indicates that there are many different kinds of Mercies for different needs. *Lamentations 3:22-23* tells us that the Mercies of God are new every morning – not evening! So, according to *Hebrews 4:16* come confidently to the Throne of God now to find Grace and Mercy in your time of need today.

Prayer: Father, in Jesus name, I pray for my eyes to be opened to understand that you O Lord God are a God of Mercy, Father, forgive all my sins by the power in the Blood of Jesus and listen to my prayer for mercy as I cry out to you for help. Keep all evil, falsehood and lies far from me today; give me neither poverty nor riches, but give me only my daily bread today and bless all the work of my hands in Jesus name. Amen.

Confession & Meditation: God is a God of Mercies and He is merciful to me.

Questions and Notes for further study:

1. What is God saying to you through this devotion and meditation?

2. What will you put into practice in your life?

Your Review after 4 weeks:

3. How has it affected your life?

4. What more could you do?

DAY 2

Scripture KJV: Colossians 2:14

"...Blotting out the handwriting of ordinances that was against us, which was contrary to us, and took it out of the way, nailing it to his cross..."

Commentary:

There are so many things that took place on the Cross which are beyond our understanding yet. God has graciously revealed some to us such as things God alone did like *2 Corinthians 5:21* – God made Jesus to be sin for us so we can be made the righteousness of God. There were things Jesus alone did like *Ephesians 2:14* - He is our Peace having made two hostile opposing groups one. There are things only the Holy Spirit did such as in *Romans 8:11* - raising Jesus from the dead. Colossians 2:14 tells exactly how God removed the rules, the laws of this world that brings sin into our lives and by which Satan our adversary uses to oppress and accuse us to us and also before God day and night.- *Revelation 12:10*. The Good news is that God has nothing against us. *Romans 8:1* - There is no condemnation for you. Today, Jesus says to you just as he said to the woman caught in adultery – *John 8:11* - Neither do I condemn you, go and sin no more.

Prayer: Heavenly Father, In Jesus name, thank you for removing the written ordinances that were against me by nailing them to the cross of my Lord Jesus. Thank you because of your mercy, you have forgiven all my sins and there is no condemnation for me. Father, through the power of your Holy Spirit, help me live a life that pleases you. Give me my daily bread, bless the works of my hands; deliver me from all evil, falsehood, lies today, in Jesus name.

Confession & Meditation: God took away all hindrances for me. I am free to serve him.

Questions and Notes for further study:

1. What is God saying to you through this devotion and meditation?

2. What will you put into practice in your life?

Your Review after 4 weeks:

3. How has it affected your life?

4. What more could you do?

DAY 3

Scripture KJV: Hebrews 12:14

"...Follow peace with all men and holiness, without which no man shall see the Lord..."

Commentary:

O there is such blessedness in Peace. God commands us in *2 Corinthians 13:11* to live in Peace. God is called the God of Peace in *Hebrews 13:20* and in *1 Thessalonians 5:23*. In *Ephesians 5:14*, Peace is listed as the Gospel of Peace - the protection for your feet in the Armour of God. *Ephesians 2:14* tells us that Jesus is our Peace. *Galatians 5:22* shows Peace as a fruit of our Spirit. How do we get peace? Live in peace? *Philippians 4: 6 -8* tells us how:

1. Pray for everything – I literally mean everything. There is no division between natural everyday things and spiritual things for a person who believes in Christ.
2. Always give Thanks with your prayers
3. *ONLY* Think on things that are *TRUE, HONEST, JUST, PURE, LOVELY, OF GOOD REPORT, VIRTUOUS, PRAISEWORTHY*

God promises in **Philippians 4:7** that if you do the above, then the peace of God, which passes all understanding, shall keep your hearts and minds through Christ Jesus.

Prayer: God of Peace, in Jesus name, thank you for Jesus and his sacrifice for me so I can have peace in my life. Father, I surrender my life to you and pray regarding everything that is going on in my life. Lord, I trust you to help me, look after me and bless me. Give me the peace of God to guard my heart and my mind today. Help me to follow peace in everything all the days of my life. Thank you for hearing me. I give you all glory in Jesus name. Amen.

Confession & Meditation: God is a God of Peace and I have his peace.

Questions and Notes for further study:

1. What is God saying to you through this devotion and meditation?

2. What will you put into practice in your life?

Your Review after 4 weeks:

3. How has it affected your life?

4. What more could you do?

DAY 4

Scripture KJV: 2 Chronicles 14:11

"...And Asa cried unto the LORD his God, and said, LORD, it is nothing with thee to help, whether with many, or with them that have no power: help us, O LORD our God; for we rest on thee, and in thy name we go against this multitude. O LORD, thou art our God; let not man prevail against thee..."

Commentary:

There is tremendous power in crying unto the Lord. Abel's blood cried out to the Lord in Genesis 4:10. God destroyed Sodom and Gomorrah because of the cries that came to him. Genesis 18:20. The Psalms are full of King David's cries to the Lord. Jesus, our Lord and our example, was heard by God the Father because of his continual fervent strong cries and tears during his life on the earth. Hebrews 5:7. Prayer is really a crying out to the Lord. He tells us in James 5:13 that if you are in any kind of trouble, you should pray (cry out) because prayer is God's **_ONLY_** way for you to get out of trouble.

Prayer: O Lord God, in Jesus name, Listen to the voice of my cry, my King, and my God: for to you I pray. Lord, it is nothing for you to help me, whether with many, or with nothing for all power is Yours. Help me, O LORD my God;

for I trust in you alone, and in your name I go through this life and against my enemies. O LORD, you are my God; do not let any evil; any of my enemies to prevail against me any day of my life, in Jesus name. Amen.

Confession & Meditation: God is my Helper and deliverer. I shall not be afraid.

Questions and Notes for further study:

1. What is God saying to you through this devotion and meditation?

2. What will you put into practice in your life?

Your Review after 4 weeks:

3. How has it affected your life?

4. What more could you do?

DAY 5

Scripture KJV: Romans 16:25.

"...power to establish you according to my gospel, and the preaching of Jesus Christ, according to the revelation of the mystery, which was kept secret since the world ... "

Commentary:

1 Corinthians 14:6 & 1 Corinthians 14:26 tells us that Revelation is **one** of the ways to help fellow Christians. False revelations magnifies people and satanic power. True revelation always magnifies Jesus, helps people and has at least 2 or 3 scriptures to support it. Revelation 1:1 shows that God gives revelation to explain to us hidden mysteries in things in the past, present or the future and always for our benefit. Romans 16:25; Galatians 1:12; Galatians 2:2; Revelation 1:1. You can learn and do things by revelation - Galatians 1:12 and Galatians 2:2. 1 Peter 1:13 tells us to be clear minded and focus on the grace coming to us at the revelation of Jesus Christ.

Prayer: O God of my Lord Jesus Christ, the Father of glory, in Jesus name, forgive all my sins. Give me the spirit of wisdom and revelation in the knowledge of you. Enlighten the eyes of my understanding to know what is the hope of your calling is, on my life. Let me know the riches of the glory of your inheritance in the saints; the exceeding greatness of your power towards me who believe, according to the working of your mighty power, which you worked in Christ, when you raised him up from the dead, and set him at your own right hand in the heavenly places. Protect me from evil today, give me my daily bread and bless all the works of my hands in Jesus name. Amen.

Confession & Meditation: I have the spirit of wisdom & revelation in the knowledge of God

Questions and Notes for further study:

1. What is God saying 0to you through this devotion and meditation?

2. What will you put into practice in your life?

Your Review after 4 weeks:

3. How has it affected your life?

4. What more could you do?

DAY 6

Scripture KJV: Acts 17:28.

"… For in him we live, and move, and have our being; as certain also of your own poets have said, for we are also his offspring…"

Commentary:

For *IN HIM* we live. Can you grasp this tremendous truth? You live in God. You move in God. You have your being in God. *Acts 17:27* says that God is *NOT FAR* from you. Think about it. God is not far from you. What does this mean to you? *Psalm 139: 2-12* gives us more details how we live, move and have our being in God. *Ephesians 5:30* informs us that we are members of his body, of his flesh, and of his bones because Jesus our Lord is the exact image of the Invisible God according to *Colossians 1:15.* So, God who is invisible has made himself visible to us through Jesus our Lord. Think on these things. Receive strength and comfort knowing that God is never far from you no matter what you are going through for God says in *Psalm 91:15* – He/she/they shall call on me, and I will answer him/her/them: I will be with him/her/them in trouble; I will deliver him/her/them:, and honor him/her/them…

Prayer: O Lord God, in Jesus name, blot out all my sins and cleanse me. Lord, I live in You. You are not far from me. Help me to live in Your Presence doing only what pleases you. Father, I am in trouble (name the trouble you are in) and You have said in Psalm 91:15 that you are with me in trouble and you will deliver me. Lord, in Jesus name, make haste now and deliver me from this trouble (name the trouble you are in) and honor me. Give me my daily bread and keep me from all evil and temptations today, in Jesus name I pray. Amen.

Confession & Meditation: God is with me and He hears and answers my prayers.

Questions and Notes for further study:

1. What is God saying to you through this devotion and meditation?

2. What will you put into practice in your life?

Your Review after 4 weeks:

3. How has it affected your life?

4. What more could you do?

DAY 7

Scripture KJV: Exodus 33:14
"...And he said, My presence shall go with you, and I will give you rest..."

Commentary:
The Presence of the Lord going with you is the first step to God giving you rest or ease. You should never go anywhere without the Presence of the Lord. *Exodus 33:15.* Why? It is because God's presence with you is the evidence that you have found favour with God and is also the proof for people to know that God is with you. *Exodus 33:16* for Glory and Honour are in the Presence of God. *1 Chronicles 16:27.* But sin makes man to hide from the presence of God. *Genesis 3:8.* Repentance of our sins is the key to staying and receiving all you need in the Presence of the Lord *Acts 3:19.* God gives rest by delivering all your enemies into your hands so that they cannot stand against you. *Joshua 21:44.* Be Strengthened Now and stay confident in the Word of God to guide your life to success always for *God's promises to you WILL NEVER FAIL TO COME TO PASS. Joshua 21:45*

Prayer: Lord God, in Jesus name, forgive all my sins. Do not cast me away from your presence and do not take your Holy Spirit from me. Hide me in the secret of your presence from the pride of man: and keep me in a pavilion from the strife of tongues all the days of my life. Let your presence go with me always and give me rest from all my enemies, all the days of my life. Give me my daily bread and keep me from all evil and temptations today, in Jesus name I pray. Amen.

Confession & Meditation: God's presence is with me and goes with me everywhere.

Questions and Notes for further study:

1. What is God saying to you through this devotion and meditation?

2. What will you put into practice in your life?

Your Review after 4 weeks:

3. How has it affected your life?

4. What more could you do?

DAY 8

Scripture KJV: Proverbs 12:15
"… The way of a fool is right in his own eyes: but he that listens to counsel is wise…"

Commentary:

We all have our own ways and although our ways are very different from one person to another, yet, God's ways are not our ways. **Isaiah 55:8.** God's ways are always right. In **Proverbs 12:15**, He refers to two kinds of people. The fool and the wise. The fool sees his ways as being right. Notice the fool is concerned with being right. But his method of being right is his own beliefs and independent thinking. Not God's word. Not other people's advice. Contrast the wise person. The wise person listens to counsel or advice of other people. They never think they know it all. They are humble. So, how do you become wise? Well, one of the ways to be wise is to walk with wise people. **Proverbs 13:20** tells you that He that walks with wise men shall be wise: but a companion of fools shall be destroyed. The other way is to ask God for wisdom according to **James 1:5** and God will give you freely.

Prayer: Heavenly Father, in Jesus name, forgive all my sins. Forgive me for not listening to your counsel and doing my own thing. Father, I realize that I am a fool and I repent.

I want to be wise so I ask you according to James 1:5 that you give me wisdom right now. Give me wisdom to act right and succeed in everything I do all the days of my life. Put wise people around me and help me to walk with them so I can be wise. Give me my daily bread. Bless the works of my hand, enlarge my territory and keep me from all evil and temptations today, in Jesus name I pray. Amen.

Confession & Meditation: God's ways are always right and I will follow him forever.

Questions and Notes for further study:

1. What is God saying to you through this devotion and meditation?

2. What will you put into practice in your life?

Your Review after 4 weeks:

3. How has it affected your life?

4. What more could you do?

DAY 9

Scripture KJV: Galatians 3:13
"... Christ has redeemed us from the curse of the law, being made a curse for us: for it is written, Cursed is every one that hangeth on a tree..."

Commentary:

Deuteronomy 28:15 – 68 details all the terrible curses God has put in place for all who do not obey his Laws. Notice Deuteronomy 28:61 where God says that every sickness etc that is not mentioned or written in the bible is a curse. But Jesus, who was sinless took on himself all our sins and all the curses of the Law mentioned above by becoming a curse for us by being hanged on a tree (cross is made from a tree) Deuteronomy 21:23. That is the reason why the blessing of Abraham and the blessings of Ephesians 1:3 is ours forever! This is so powerful because this is the reason why you will succeed; why your family will live, be in health and prosper and why your prayers will work. Get this inside you. Meditate upon. Declare it. Speak it day and night until it becomes a living reality inside you and you will prosper and succeed in life. All of this, is because of Jesus. Glory to his name forever!

Prayer: Lord God of Hosts, in Jesus name, forgive all my sins. Thank you that Jesus became a curse for me so that

I can receive the blessings of God therefore according to Deuteronomy 28 (name your problem or sickness here) is a curse of the law but according to Galatians 3:13 I am redeemed from all the curses of the law. In Jesus name, I am set free and healed of (*name your problem or sickness here*). Give me my daily bread. Bless the works of my hand, enlarge my territory and keep me from all evil and temptations today, in Jesus name.

Confession & Meditation: Christ's blood has redeemed me from every curse.

Questions and Notes for further study:

1. What is God saying to you through this devotion and meditation?

2. What will you put into practice in your life?

Your Review after 4 weeks:

3. How has it affected your life?

4. What more could you do?

DAY 10

Scripture KJV: Genesis 1:1
"... In the beginning God created the heaven and the earth..."

Commentary:

John 1:1 tells us that In the beginning was the Word, and the Word was with God, and the Word was God. The Word i.e. Jesus was made flesh. **John 1:14**. All things created in heaven, the earth, visible and invisible, whether they be thrones, or dominions, or principalities, or powers were created by Jesus, and for Jesus. We understand the worlds (explains the solar systems and multitudes of galaxies out there) were framed by the word of God and that what we see was made by who we do not see. Paul calls him the Invisible God. **Colossians 1:15**. We know from **Romans 4:17** that God gives life to the dead (raised Jesus from the dead; Lazarus etc etc) and calls into life things that do not yet exist (feeding the 5 thousand and other miracles) – we understand all this through faith. **Hebrews 11:3**. Is there anything dead in your life? Is there anything you need that does not yet exist?

Prayer: Lord God, in Jesus name, cleanse me of all my sins. I praise you my Creator and give you glory. Father (tell God the problems here) and I don't know what to do but my eyes are on you for my help comes from you. Father, give life to (name whatever that is dead in your life) and bring into existence now (name the things you want God to bring into existence for you) in the name of Jesus. Lord, give me my daily bread. Bless the works of my hand and protect me from all evil and temptations today, in Jesus name I pray. Amen.

Confession & Meditation: The God who created the heavens and the earth is my Father.

Questions and Notes for further study:

1. What is God saying to you through this devotion and meditation?

2. What will you put into practice in your life?

Your Review after 4 weeks:

3. How has it affected your life?

4. What more could you do?

DAY 11

Scripture KJV: Matthew 11:28

"...Come to Me, all who are weary and heavy-laden, and I will give you rest..."

Commentary:

Mathew 11:28 is talking to those who are weary, tired and burdened with the cares and worries of life, finances, troubles. Jesus says that the solution is come to HIM. Why? **Matthew 11:27** tells us that ALL THINGS has been given to Jesus.. **Psalm 23: 1** tells us that The Lord is our Shepherd. Notice that we are not our own shepherd. **Proverbs 3:5** tells us that we are to trust in the Lord with our heart and not lean on our understanding. Here in **Matthew 11:28** Jesus says we are to come to him. How do you come to Jesus? You come to Jesus by believing in him, that He is who he says he is and by following his words – the bible and praying always to God the Father in Jesus name. That's how you come to Jesus. What do you do with worries, cares, burdens, troubles? You do what 1 Peter 5:7 says: Cast them all upon Jesus because He cares for you as your Shepherd and he will give you rest.

Prayer: In Jesus name, Father God, forgive all my sins. Lord I have many cares, troubles and worries (list them to God). You have said that I should cast them all to you. I now cast them all on you for you are my Shepherd and you love me and care for me. Lord God, work everything out well for me. Let everything turn out well for me. I don't know how but I know you are The Almighty God and you have all power and there is nothing you cannot do. Thank you. Lord, give me my daily bread. Bless the works of my hand and protect me from all evil and temptations today, in Jesus name I pray. Amen.

Confession & Meditation: I cast my cares on Jesus and He gives me rest.

Questions and Notes for further study:

1. What is God saying to you through this devotion and meditation?

2. What will you put into practice in your life?

Your Review after 4 weeks:

3. How has it affected your life?

4. What more could you do?

DAY 12

Scripture KJV: Matthew 11:29

"... Take My yoke upon you and learn from Me, for I am gentle and humble in heart, and you will find rest for your souls..."

Commentary:

Our Lord Jesus advises us to learn from him. If we are wise, we will do just that for He knows all things. **1 John 3:20**. Gentleness and humility in your heart is **THE KEY** to finding rest for your soul (your mind, your emotions and your will). Notice Jesus said **"in heart"** and **"for your souls"**. So, your heart and your soul are not the same. According to **1 Thessalonians 5:23**. You are a 3 part being. Spirit, Soul and Body. With your Spirit, (the hidden man of the heart. **1 Peter 3:4**) you interact with the Spiritual World. With your Soul you interact with the Mental World (**Romans 12:2**). With your Body you interact with this Physical World. (**Romans 6:12**) All of these take place simultaneously and seamlessly so we are not often aware of it happening. Gentleness is a fruit of your Spirit (your heart) .**Galatians 5:22.** God's ONLY way is for His Word (Jesus), who is a Spirit, to be received by your spirit. Your spirit is meant to live the Word (Jesus) through faith, to rule your mind, your body and your life – The God Kind of Life.

Prayer: Heavenly Father, forgive all my sins. Your Word says I am to be gentle and humble in heart so I can find rest for my soul. Lord, help me learn to be gentle and humble in everything. Guide me. Lead me. Teach me your ways. Lord, give me my daily bread. Bless the works of my hand and protect me from all evil and temptations today, in Jesus name I pray. Amen.

Confession & Meditation: I take Jesus's yoke of humility and gentleness on me.

Questions and Notes for further study:

1. What is God saying to you through this devotion and meditation?

2. What will you put into practice in your life?

Your Review after 4 weeks:

3. How has it affected your life?

4. What more could you do?

DAY 13

Scripture KJV: Matthew 8:7
"...And Jesus said to him, I will come and HEAL him..."

Commentary:
This was Jesus reply to the Centurion request for the healing of his servant. Note the Centurion was not sick. He was praying for his employee who was sick. Jairus the Ruler of the Synagogue prayed for healing of his sick daughter. **Matthew 9:18-19**. Peter wife's mother was healed in **Matthew 8:14**. We learn from these scriptures that we can pray for another person's healing just as easily as we can for our own healing. **Matthew 20:30**. God creates the fruit of your lips; and heals every sickness and every disease. **Isaiah 57:19; Mathew 9:35**. All healing is based on Jesus taking our infirmities and sins upon his body **Isaiah 53:4-5; Matthew 8:17**, and how did He do that, exactly? He did so by his stripes, we *were* healed. **1 Peter 2:24**. How do we get our healing? The same way we got our salvation – by believing God's word in our hearts; confessing God's word with our mouth **Romans 10:9-10** and keeping God's words before our eyes. **Proverbs 4:21.**

Prayer: Lord God, have mercy on me. I forgive all who has hurt me. Forgive all my sins. Thank you that it is by the stripes of Jesus, I was healed. I believe your Word and receive my healing from (*name what the sickness is*) now in Jesus name. In Jesus name, I command this sickness to leave me and never return. I declare I am healthy, well, strong and whole all the days of my life. Lord, guide me. Lead me. Teach me your ways. Lord, give me my daily bread. Bless the works of my hand and protect me from all evil and temptations. Amen.

Confession & Meditation: Jesus lives in me and has healed me by his stripes.

Questions and Notes for further study:

1. What is God saying to you through this devotion and meditation?

2. What will you put into practice in your life?

Your Review after 4 weeks:

3. How has it affected your life?

4. What more could you do?

DAY 14

Scripture KJV: Matthew 4:23

"... And Jesus went about all Galilee, teaching in their synagogues, and preaching the gospel of the kingdom, and healing all manner of sickness and all manner of disease among the people..."

Commentary:

Our Lord's business was teaching, preaching and healing. Notice Jesus healed ALL manner of sickness and disease. Notice there is a distinction between sickness and disease. There are not the same. However, Jesus healed both of them equally. Let's look at a practical example of the healing of a man with an incurable skin disease of leprosy. Notice what the man did. First, he worshipped Jesus. Secondly, he asked Jesus to cleanse him. (Cleansing is also a form of healing). Jesus responded to that man's faith and cleansed or healed him. Matthew 8: 2-4. We learn from **Hebrews 13:8** that Jesus is the same **yesterday** (what he did in **Matthew 4:23**); **today** (if you or anyone need healing from any sickness or disease); and **tomorrow** (if you need healing tomorrow).Jesus saves and heals you to the uttermost. **Hebrews 7:25.**

Prayer: Lord God, have mercy on me and Forgive all my sins. I forgive everyone who has offended me. Thank you that it is by the stripes of Jesus, I was healed. I believe your Word and receive my healing from (**name what the sickness is**) now in Jesus name. In Jesus name, I command this sickness to leave me and never return. I declare I am healthy, well, strong and whole all the days of my life. Lord, guide me. Lead me. Teach me your ways. Lord, give me my daily bread. Bless the works of my hand and protect me from all evil temptations. Amen.

Confession & Meditation: Jesus is my healer. He lives in me and healed me by his stripes.

Questions and Notes for further study:

1. What is God saying to you through this devotion and meditation?

2. What will you put into practice in your life?

Your Review after 4 weeks:

3. How has it affected your life?

4. What more could you do?

DAY 15

Scripture KJV: John 17:8

"... For I have given to them the WORDS which you gave me; and they have received them, and have known surely that I came out from you, and they have believed that you did send me..."

Commentary:

Our Lord Jesus prayed for us in John 17. His prayer is that we all may be ONE even as he and The Father are one. How do we become one? By loving each other and obeying all the WORDS Jesus gave us. In Matthew 5:44 and John 15:12-13, one of the words of Jesus to us is to love God, love our enemies, bless them that curse us, do good to them that hate us, and pray for them that spitefully use us, and persecute us. This is Love in action. 1 Corinthians 13 tells us that Love is the most excellent way for love does not work any evil to anyone. Romans 13:10 and without love you are nothing. Even Faith works by Love. Galatians 5:6. We have the Love of God in our hearts so we can love like God loves. Romans 5:4. Love is always kind. We all need to be kinder every day to people; fellow Christians and our enemies for no one is perfect yet.

Prayer: Lord God, Forgive all my sins as I have forgiven all who offended me. Thank you that your love is shed abroad in my heart and I can walk in love. Lord, give me revelation of how to walk in love towards my enemies and those I come in contact with. Lord, Guide me. Lead me. Teach me your ways. Lord, give me my daily bread. Bless the works of my hand and protect me from all evil and temptations today, in Jesus name I pray. Amen.

Confession & Meditation: Jesus was sent by God to save me and help me walk in love.

Questions and Notes for further study:

1. What is God saying to you through this devotion and meditation?

2. What will you put into practice in your life?

Your Review after 4 weeks:

3. How has it affected your life?

4. What more could you do?

DAY 16

Scripture KJV: Mark 13:31

"... Heaven and earth shall pass away: but my WORDS shall not pass away..."

Commentary:

Can you see this? This Heaven and This earth shall pass away BUT Jesus words shall not pass away. **Luke 21:33.** The laws of nature affects every part of our lives i.e. everything and everyone grows old. In comparison, the words of Jesus shall not pass away or ever grow old. Why? It is because his Words are SPIRIT and they are LIFE. **John 6:63**. They are SUPERNATURAL words. Note that everything God made, he made through words. **Genesis 1.** It is still through words, the universe and solar system and our lives are upheld. **Hebrews 1:3**. Even our salvation (Eternal life, healing, deliverance etc etc) comes through words. **Romans 1:16; John 6:68.** So, knowing how powerful words are, start to monitor your words What words are you speaking?. Are you speaking words of death? Or are you speaking the words of Jesus in your situation? Jesus words will always work and triumph over anything because his words are SUPERNATURAL so TRUST IN HIS WORDS and speak life!

Prayer: Father, Forgive all my sins as I have forgiven all who offended me. I accept your words as the words of eternal life. You came that I may have life and life more abundantly. I confess Jesus died for my sins and rose again for my justification. I accept Jesus as my Lord and Savior. I receive your eternal life into my spirit right now. Lord, Guide me. Lead me. Teach me your ways. Lord, give me my daily bread. Bless the works of my hand and protect me from all evil and temptations today, in Jesus name I pray. Amen.

Confession & Meditation: The Words of Jesus are Spirit and Life to my life.

Questions and Notes for further study:

1. What is God saying to you through this devotion and meditation?

2. What will you put into practice in your life?

Your Review after 4 weeks:

3. How has it affected your life?

4. What more could you do?

DAY 17

Scripture KJV: Luke 24:11

"...And their words seemed to them as idle tales, and they believed them not..."

Commentary:

Two things can result when we speak to another person. Either they believe us or they do not believe us. This passage of scripture gives one reason why people may not believe us, which is, that our words may seem to people as idle tales i.e. fantasy. Notice that people may not believe us even though we are telling the truth even though logic, human nature and common sense says that if we are telling the truth, surely we must be believed? Well, No. Not really. I am sure in your personal life, you have come across this quirk of human nature that can cause innocent people to be killed, punished, and their lives destroyed because you were not believed, even though you were telling the truth. Jesus prayed in John 17 for those of us who would believe in him because of the words of the Apostles. Jesus blessed us who believed because of the words of Peter, John, Mark, Paul etc etc. John 20:29. This contradicts the common saying – "seeing is believing" i.e. doubting Thomas. Jesus seems to be saying – "believing is seeing"

Prayer: Father, Forgive all my sins as I have forgiven all who offended me. I believe the words of your disciples. Open my mind to understand them and apply them in my life. Thank you that I am blessed so help me live for you according to these words of eternal life. Lord, Guide me. Lead me. Teach me your ways. Lord and give me my daily bread. Bless the works of my hand and protect me from all evil and temptations today, in Jesus name I pray. Amen.

Confession & Meditation: The Words of Jesus are Spirit and Life and I believe them.

Questions and Notes for further study:

1. What is God saying to you through this devotion and meditation?

2. What will you put into practice in your life?

Your Review after 4 weeks:

3. How has it affected your life?

4. What more could you do?

DAY 18

Scripture KJV: Daniel 10:12

"... Then said he to me, Fear not, Daniel: for from the first day that you did set your heart to understand, and to chasten yourself before your God, your WORDS were heard, and I am come for your words..."

Commentary:

Here God reveals what happens when we pray. First you pray using words. Notice, God hears you the first time you pray but the answer usually does not come immediately. Daniel had to wait for 21 days. But notice the two things Daniel did. He set his heart to understand. Then he chastened himself before God i.e. he fasted. All this happened because Daniel learned from the word of God Daniel about the promise of God to Israel. **Daniel 9:2.** *YOUR PRAYERS MUST BE BASED ON THE WORD OF GOD*. **James 5:16** tells us that the prayers of a righteous man avails much. **Romans 5:17** tells us that righteousness is a free gift from God, given to those who believe and live by his Word. **Genesis 15:6; Romans 4:3.** God is no respecter of persons. **Acts 10:34. So, be** encouraged for God will answer your prayers!

Prayer: Father, Forgive all my sins as I have forgiven all who offended me. Thank you Lord for saving me, giving me abundance of grace and the gift of righteousness. Lord, on these grounds, I ask you for (*put your personal prayer requests here – write it down in a prayer journal so you can cross it off when you receive the answer as a testimony to share with other people how God heard your prayers*). Lord, Guide me. Lead me. Teach me your ways and give me my daily bread. Bless the works of my hand and protect me from all evil and temptations in Jesus name.

Confession & Meditation: God is no respecter of persons. He hears & answers my prayers.

Questions and Notes for further study:

1. What is God saying to you through this devotion and meditation?

2. What will you put into practice in your life?

Your Review after 4 weeks:

3. How has it affected your life?

4. What more could you do?

DAY 19

Scripture KJV: Mark 16:15

"... And he said to them, Go you into all the world, and preach the gospel to every creature..."

Commentary:

This is a command to us all. **Acts 10:42**. Jesus said *you* go and preach the kingdom of God. **Luke 9:60**. We are to preach the gospel daily. **Act 5:42**. What is the Gospel? It is teaching and preaching Jesus Christ and that He is the Judge of the living and the dead. **Acts 10:42**. The Gospel is also the Power of God unto salvation. **Romans 1:16**. God will hold us accountable for the souls of the people who went to hell and were cast into the lake of fire because we did not preach the gospel to them. Hell is real. **Matthew 5:29-30**. The Lake of Fire is real. **Revelation 20:15**. Anyone in there is tormented day and night for all eternity. **Revelation 20:10**. We are to preach the gospel. **We are never to force people to believe**. Some people will not believe. Don't let that bother you at all. It is their choice. There are many that will believe and for them, it is all worth it. God said it those who CHOOSE to believe in Jesus that will have everlasting life. **John 3:16.** There is much joy in heaven over ONE person who repents. Start today to bring heaven joy by preaching Jesus to someone.

Prayer: Father, Forgive me for not preaching the gospel. Give me boldness to preach the gospel. Let me be a Christian who brings great joy to heaven all the days of my life. Lord, give me my daily bread. bless the works of my hand. Protect me from all evil and temptations today, in Jesus name I pray. Amen.

Confession & Meditation: I am bold to preach the gospel to everyone.

Questions and Notes for further study:

1. What is God saying to you through this devotion and meditation?

2. What will you put into practice in your life?

Your Review after 4 weeks:

3. How has it affected your life?

4. What more could you do?

DAY 20

Scripture KJV: Romans 4:21

"...And being fully persuaded that, what HE had promised, HE was able also to perform..."

Commentary:

This is the crux of what Faith is. You have to be fully persuaded of God's promises applicable to your situation to see answers to your prayers and live a successful Christian life. What does being fully persuaded mean? Persuade itself is a verb. It is an active word, a doing word. Not a passive word. It means to win over someone to take a particular course of action. And winning them over by using *reason, logic and emotion.* **Acts 18:4.** Paul reasoned and persuaded the Jews and the Greeks. Then, there is the evil side of persuasion. **Matthew 27:20.** The chief priests and elders persuaded the multitude to ask for Barabbas, and destroy Jesus. But thank God that satan won a battle there but Jesus won the war for us. So, how do you become fully persuaded? Long patience without being angry. **Proverbs 25:15.** How do you start? By meditating on God's words (the Power of God. **Romans 1:16**) day and night. **Joshua 1:8; 1Timothy 4:15.** To do so, you will need to have patience with yourself.

Prayer: Father, forgive my sins. I forgive everyone who has hurt me. Lord, I learn that I have to be fully persuaded of your promises by meditating on your words. Help me to meditate on your words with patience so my profiting may be evident to all. Give me understanding of your words and help me put them into practice today. Lord, give me my daily bread. Bless the works of my hand and protect me from all evil and temptations today, in Jesus name.

Confession & Meditation: God is able to perform everything He promised to me.

Questions and Notes for further study:

1. What is God saying to you through this devotion and meditation?

2. What will you put into practice in your life?

Your Review after 4 weeks:

3. How has it affected your life?

4. What more could you do?

DAY 21

Scripture KJV: Matthew 1:1

"...The book of the generation of Jesus Christ, the son of David, the son of Abraham..."

Commentary:

The world gives every generation a name. Generation X, Generation Y, MTV Generation etc etc. God calls the gospel of Matthew the book of the generation of Jesus Christ. God describes Jesus as the son of David, the son of Abraham. **Luke 1:32.** Notice what language God uses. He said 'the son' He didn't say 'a son'. Why is Jesus 'the son' of David? Well, God promised David that he will never lack a successor to sit on his throne forever. **Jeremiah 23:5; Isaiah 9:7.** Then **Isaiah 9:6** goes into great details about this SON of David. He will rule the earth forever as King of Kings and Lord of Lords. **Revelation 19:16.** He is the Wonderful Counselor (not just any counselor!), Mighty God, Eternal Father, Prince of Peace. There will be no end to His government of justice and righteousness. Meditate on these facts for you are in Jesus. How? Because you are a new creation. **2 Corinthians 5:17** So, Wait on the LORD: be of good courage, and he shall strengthen your heart: wait, I say, on the LORD. **Psalm 27:14.** *God will NEVER fail you.* **Deuteronomy 31:6**

Prayer: Father, forgive my sins. I forgive everyone who has offended me. Lord God, the son of David, Mighty God, Eternal Father and Prince of Peace. Help me to know you more for without you, I am nothing. Give me a hunger for you, for righteousness and for the things of God. Strengthen my heart and help me love like you today. Lord, give me my daily bread. Bless the works of my hand. Keep me safe from all evil and all temptations in Jesus name.

Confession & Meditation: Jesus, the son of David and Abraham is my savior and shepherd.

Questions and Notes for further study:

1. What is God saying to you through this devotion and meditation?

2. What will you put into practice in your life?

Your Review after 4 weeks:

3. How has it affected your life?

4. What more could you do?

DAY 22

Scripture KJV: Proverbs 12:11
"...He that tilleth his land shall be satisfied with bread but He that follows vain persons in void of understanding..."

Commentary:

God tells us that it is by hard work we will be successful in our jobs and business. That will never change. The result of that hard work is that you will not go hungry. Proverbs 22:29. But your hard work has to have the blessing of God upon it for it is the Blessing of God that makes you rich. Proverbs 10:22 Notices Jesus redeemed us from the curse but he did so through work. John 9:4. God himself worked. Genesis 1; God›s work is for you to believe in Jesus. John 6:29. Paul says if you don›t work, you don›t eat. 2 Thessalonians 3:10. We can expect fruitfulness and prosperity from our work because every work of our hands is blessed. Deuteronomy 28: 8. Galatians 3:10. Do you need a job, better job or business of your own? Ask God and it shall be given to you. Since, it is God›s will for you to work, do you think He will refuse to answer your prayers? Of course not!

Prayer: Father, forgive my sins. I forgive everyone who has offended me. Thank you Lord for blessing me with every spiritual blessing. Lord, give me a very well paid job (or business, if that's you wish) I will work hard on my job or business to bring Glory to you. Lord, give me my daily bread. Bless the works of my hand and keep me safe from all evil and all temptations today, in Jesus name I pray. Amen.

Confession & Meditation: I do not follow vain persons. I follow the word of God faithfully.

Questions and Notes for further study:

1. What is God saying to you through this devotion and meditation?

2. What will you put into practice in your life?

Your Review after 4 weeks:

3. How has it affected your life?

4. What more could you do?

DAY 23

Scripture KJV: Matthew 1:21

"... And she shall bring forth a son, and you shall call his name JESUS: for he shall save his people from their sins..."

Commentary:

The Word of an Angel of the Lord is steadfast. **Hebrews 2:2.** Everything about the birth of Jesus was done to fulfil what God said through Prophet Isaiah several hundred years ago prior to the birth of Jesus. **Isaiah 7:14.** In **2 Chronicles 20:20**, we learn that if we believe God, we shall be established. If we believe his prophets, we shall prosper. Note the name Jesus was given by God and not men. In fact, Jesus, as far as the Bible is concerned, is the **_SECOND_** person God named before his birth. **Luke 2:21.** The other being John the Baptist. Everyone else had their original names changed by God. **Genesis 17:5.** We too will have a new name. **Revelation 2:17. The name of Jesus is the most powerful name.** We are children of God through Jesus and must do everything in his name. **Galatians 2:26. Colossians 3:17.** We defeat Satan and the kingdom of darkness in Jesus name. **Luke 10:19; Mark 16:17; Acts 16:18; James 4:17.** Why? Because every knee (Satan's knee included) in heaven, the earth and under the earth must bow at the name of Jesus. **Philippians 2:9-10.**

Prayer: Father, forgive my sins. I forgive everyone who has offended me. In the name of Jesus, I command every work of Satan in my life to be defeated and destroyed. In the name of Jesus, I recover everything Satan has stolen from me. Lord, restore to me the years the locust, caterpillar and worm has eaten. Lord, give me my daily bread. Bless the works of my hand and keep me safe from all evil and all temptations today, in Jesus name I pray. Amen.

Confession & Meditation: Jesus is the only one to save me from my sins.

Questions and Notes for further study:

1. What is God saying to you through this devotion and meditation?

2. What will you put into practice in your life?

Your Review after 4 weeks:

3. How has it affected your life?

4. What more could you do?

DAY 24

Scripture KJV: Matthew 1:18
"... Now the birth of Jesus Christ was on this wise: When as his mother Mary was espoused to Joseph, before they came together, she was found with Child of the Holy Ghost..."

Commentary:

Jesus is called the Child of the Holy Ghost. Who is the Holy Ghost? He is a Divine Person. He is God. **1John 5:7.** He speaks. **John 16:13. Act 13:2. Hebrews 3:7.** He feels. **Ephesians 4:30.** He teaches. **John 14:26, 1 Corinthians 2:13.** Everything of God that I know, write and speak now and in the future are what the Holy Ghost has taught me. He is so special and unique. All manner of evil words against Jesus can be forgiven but evil words against The Holy Ghost shall never be forgiven. **Matthew 12:31-32.** Your body is his Temple. **1 Corinthians 6:19.** The Holy Ghost is God's witness to your heart. **Act 15:8.** Why is He in you? So you can be witness to Jesus. **Act 1:8.** How? By signs following – casting out devils; speaking with new tongues; healing; neutralizing poisons; Mark **16:17-18.** Our Lord Jesus works with us to confirm his words with signs. **Mark 16:20.**

Prayer: Father, forgive my sins. I forgive everyone who has offended me. Lord Jesus, baptize me with the Holy Ghost and with power to bear witness to you in all the earth with signs following. Fill me with your Holy Spirit and teach me to know you intimately. Lord, give me my daily bread. Lead and Guide me. Bless me and bless all the works of my hand. Father, keep me safe from all evil and from all temptations today, in Jesus name.

Confession & Meditation: The Words of Jesus are Spirit and Life to my life.

Questions and Notes for further study:

1. What is God saying to you through this devotion and meditation?

2. What will you put into practice in your life?

Your Review after 4 weeks:

3. How has it affected your life?

4. What more could you do?

DAY 25

Scripture KJV: Luke 1:37
"... For with God nothing shall be impossible..."

Commentary:
The birth of Jesus demonstrates that NOTHING is impossible with God. The Angel Gabriel said to Mary that nothing is impossible with God. Jesus repeated that nothing is impossible with God. Matthew 19:26. Notice the key here – *"...with God..."* not with man. How are things made possible with God? By your believing in God – if you can believe. Mark 9:23. How did the birth of Jesus come about? By Mary believing the Word of God as delivered by The Angel Gabriel. For a Virgin to have a child without sexual intercourse is impossible. But the birth of Jesus proves that nothing is impossible with God. Now, by modern medical science via artificial insemination, we know babies can now be born without sexual intercourse – proving God's word as true. In the case of Mary, God did it all by his Spirit. Zechariah 4:6. Do you have a situation that seems impossible? Pray and give thanks until the answer comes. 1Thessalonians 5:17.

Prayer: Father, forgive my sins. I forgive everyone who has offended me. Father, your word says that nothing is impossible with God. Lord, I pray concerning (now *present* *your requests here)* Lord, these requests may seem impossible to men but not impossible with you O God. Father, grant my requests quickly. Fill me with your Holy Spirit and teach me to know you. Lord, give me my daily bread. Lead and Guide me. Bless me in Jesus name.

Confession & Meditation: Nothing is impossible with God. Nothing is impossible for God.

Questions and Notes for further study:

1. What is God saying to you through this devotion and meditation?

2. What will you put into practice in your life?

Your Review after 4 weeks:

3. How has it affected your life?

4. What more could you do?

DAY 26

Scripture KJV: Luke 1:41

"... And it came to pass, that, when Elisabeth heard the salutation of Mary, the babe leaped in her womb; and Elisabeth was filled with the Holy Ghost..."

Commentary:

Mary was visited by The Angel Gabriel. Notice the supernatural events that followed the angelic visitation. The voice of Mary was enough to trigger the filling of John the Baptist with the Holy Spirit right from his mother's womb thus showing, yet again, that nothing is impossible for God! Notice Elisabeth had to hear Mary's voice in order for the supernatural events to take place. So, also we have to hear God's voice for faith comes by hearing and hearing by the word of God. Romans 10:17. Remember that Faith is an invisible substance. Hebrews 11:1. That substance is the word of God that creates the answer to that which you pray for. Everything about Jesus birth was impossible to man but possible with God. Do you have a situation that seems impossible and you have tried everything? Now, take God at his word and bring before him your prayer requests and He promises to answer. Luke 11:9

Prayer: Father, forgive my sins. I forgive everyone who has offended me. Father, your word says that nothing is impossible with God. Lord, I pray (now **present your requests here**) Lord, these requests may seem impossible to men but not impossible with you O God. Father, grant my requests quickly. Fill me with your Holy Spirit and teach me to know you. Lord, give me my daily bread. Lead and Guide me. Bless me and bless all the works of my hand.

Confession & Meditation: What is impossible for man is possible for God.

Questions and Notes for further study:

1. What is God saying to you through this devotion and meditation?

2. What will you put into practice in your life?

Your Review after 4 weeks:

3. How has it affected your life?

4. What more could you do?

DAY 27

Scripture KJV: Luke 2:7
"...And she gave birth to her firstborn, a son. She wrapped him in cloths and placed him in a manger because there was no room for them at the in..."

Commentary:
Jesus is born. The invisible God became visible. Notice that the birth was Jesus was normal. Just like the birth of you and me. This shows us that God uses both the supernatural and the natural in dealing with us and in answering our prayers. Many people forget this when waiting for answers to their prayers. Take for example healing. God supernatural promise is that by the wounds of Jesus, you ARE healed. 1 Peter 2:24. In some cases, people are healed instantaneously. Others are healed when you go to the Doctor or hospital and take medicines. Is it still God at work in both ways? Yes. He is our Healer. Exodus 15:26. Note also that Mary had to go through the pains of labour and childbirth. This tells us that even if we have the supernatural word of promise of God and we believe it, we still have a part to play in its fulfilment. It is not magic. You have to work at it and do everything naturally necessary on your part. That is why Paul tells us to WORK out our salvation with trembling and fear. Philippians 2:12. The work we have to do is to believe God and act in line with

what God has told us. For example, the first miracle Jesus did was where He changed water into wine at the wedding feast. He told them what to do in the natural i.e. bring lots of water and take the water to be tasted. John 2:5-11. The formula for success in life is to do what He tells you to do.

Prayer: Father, forgive my sins. I forgive everyone who has offended me. Father, your word says that nothing is impossible with God. Lord, I pray concerning *(now present your requests here)* Lord, these requests may seem impossible to men but not impossible with you O God. Father, grant my requests quickly. Fill me with your Holy Spirit and teach me to know you intimately. Lord, give me my daily bread. Lead and Guide me. Bless me and bless all the works of my hand. Father, keep me safe from all evil and temptations today, in Jesus name.

Confession & Meditation: I do what Jesus says and I receive my miracle.

Questions and Notes for further study:

1. What is God saying to you through this devotion and meditation?

2. What will you put into practice in your life?

Your Review after 4 weeks:

3. How has it affected your life?

4. What more could you do?

DAY 29

Scripture KJV: Mathew 2:1

"... Now when Jesus was born in Bethlehem of Judaea in the days of Herod the king, behold, there came wise men..."

Commentary:

Wise men have been described in the Bible as being of many kinds. In **Genesis 41:8** and **Daniel 4:6**, they are described as men who can interpret a King's dream. In **Exodus 7:11**, they are men who can perform spell and enchantments to imitate all the miracles that God did against Pharaoh in Egypt. They are described as rulers. **Deuteronomy 1:13-15.** The wise men were not ordinary men. They were very rich and influential, schooled in the wisdom of this world on which our civilization, school systems and all our learning depends on. *But is the world's wisdom same as God's wisdom?* **1 Corinthians 1:20**. No. God calls the world's wisdom foolish. **1 Corinthians 1:21**. Due to the wisdom of this world, Millions consider the message of Jesus as foolishness. *What does God call wisdom?* Wisdom is a Spirit. **Isaiah 11:2.** Jesus is called the Wisdom of God. **1 Corinthians 1:24**. God is saying prophetically through the story of the wise men that even the wisdom of this world has to bow to Jesus.

Prayer: Based on Ephesians 1:17; Isaiah 11:2

Father, forgive my sins. I forgive everyone who has offended me. Father, give me the Spirit of Wisdom and Revelation in the knowledge of you. Help me be wise to make wise decisions. Lord, give me my daily bread. Lead and Guide me. Bless me and bless all the works of my hand. Father, keep me safe from all evil and from all temptations in Jesus name.

Confession & Meditation: Jesus is the wisdom of God for me.

Questions and Notes for further study:

1. What is God saying to you through this devotion and meditation?

2. What will you put into practice in your life?

Your Review after 4 weeks:

3. How has it affected your life?

4. What more could you do?

DAY 30

Scripture KJV: Luke 2:22 -24

"… And when the days of her purification according to the Law of Moses were accomplished, they brought him to Jerusalem, to present him to the Lord; (As it is written in the law of the LORD, Every male that opens the womb shall be called holy to the Lord;) And to offer a sacrifice according to that which is said in the law of the Lord…"

Commentary:

Notice Jesus, even though he was God, still had to be presented to God according to the Law of Moses. **Why**? To show us an example that we are never above the law of God no matter whether we are new creations as in **2 Corinthians 5:17** or sitting in heavenly places in Christ according to **Ephesians 2:6**. Notwithstanding our authority and place in Christ, we are still required to obey the Laws of God. Jesus gave us two laws. Love God with all your heart, soul and body. **Mark 12:30**. Then love your neighbor (including your enemies) as yourself. **Luke 6:35. John 13:34.** We are to keep these commandments by the help of the Holy Spirit. *What does loving God look like?* **John 14: 21.** You see how essential it is to ask for forgiveness daily because not many of us love God, our neighbor or our enemies like Jesus commanded?

Prayer: Father, forgive my sins. I forgive everyone who has offended me. Father, help me love you according to your commands. Help me love my neighbor and my enemies according to your commandment. Help me to be wise and make wise decisions every day. Lord, give me my daily bread. Lead and Guide me. Bless me and bless all the works of my hand. Father, keep me safe from all evil and from all temptations today, in Jesus name I pray. Amen.

Confession & Meditation: I love God with all my heart, soul and body.

Questions and Notes for further study:

1. What is God saying to you through this devotion and meditation?

2. What will you put into practice in your life?

Your Review after 4 weeks:

3.   How has it affected your life?

4.   What more could you do?

DAY 31

Scripture KJV: Luke 2:25 -32

"... And, behold, there was a man in Jerusalem, whose name was Simeon; and the same man was just and devout ...And it was revealed to him by the Holy Ghost, that he should not see death, before he had seen the Lord's Christ. And he came by the Spirit into the temple... for my eyes have seen your salvation, which you have prepared before the face of all people; A light to lighten the Gentiles, and the glory of your people Israel... "

Commentary:

Notice one of the many manifestations of the Holy Ghost. Here, he revealed to Simeon that he would see Jesus before he died. Notice that the Holy Ghost prompted him to go into the temple on the same day Jesus was eight days old and was being presented. Notice also that Simeon called Jesus – God's salvation. He also called Jesus, a Light to lighten the Gentiles (us), and the glory of Israel. Simeon is another witness to the birth of Jesus. Remember Mary is the first witness. Joseph is the second witness. The Shepherds were the third witness. The wise men were the fourth witness. Simeon is the fifth witness. The Angels were also witnesses. Elizabeth the cousin of Mary was another witness.

Prayer: Father, forgive my sins. I forgive everyone who has offended me. Father, I believe the witness of the birth of Jesus through Mary, Joseph, The Shepherds, the wise men, Simeon and the Angels and accept Jesus as my Lord. Lord, give me my daily bread. Lead and Guide me. Bless me. Bless all the works of my hand and keep me safe from all evil in Jesus name.

Confession & Meditation: The Words of Jesus are Spirit and Life to my life.

Questions and Notes for further study:

1. What is God saying to you through this devotion and meditation?

2. What will you put into practice in your life?

Your Review after 4 weeks:

3. How has it affected your life?

4. What more could you do?

DAY 32

Scripture KJV: Luke 2:36-38

"...And there was one Anna, a prophetess, the daughter of Phanuel, of the tribe of Aser: she was of a great age... And she was a widow of about fourscore and four years, which departed not from the temple, but served God with fastings and prayers night and day. And she coming in that instant gave thanks likewise to the Lord, and spoke of him to all them that looked for redemption in Jerusalem..."

Commentary:

Look at yet another witness to Jesus. Notice Anna was a prophetess – someone who is God's spokesperson. Notice she served God by fastings and prayers night and day. *Ask yourself, how are you serving God?* Fastings and prayers are one of the MOST powerful ways to serve God and see answers to your prayers. Anna was always in the temple. She was always in the Church. This tells you that you cannot neglect Church. Church is where Jesus is. It is where two or three are gathered in the name of Jesus. Church is not a physical building. Anna's timing was perfect. *What did she do?* She gave thanks to God and spoke of him to people.

Prayer: Father, I forgive everyone who has offended me and pray you to forgive my sins. Father, thank you for sending my Lord Jesus to redeem me from my sins and give me eternal life. Give me boldness to speak to everyone about you. Give me strength to achieve all my goals and objectives in life. Help me be wise and make wise decisions every day. Lord, give me my daily bread. Lead and Guide me. Bless me and bless all the works of my hand. Father, keep me safe from all evil and from all temptations today, in Jesus name I pray. Amen.

Confession & Meditation: I speak about Jesus to everyone and they listen to me.

Questions and Notes for further study:

1. What is God saying to you through this devotion and meditation?

2. What will you put into practice in your life?

Your Review after 4 weeks:

3. How has it affected your life?

4. What more could you do?

DAY 33

Scripture KJV: Luke 1:31

"... And, behold, you shall conceive in your womb, and bring forth a son, and shall call his name JESUS..."

Commentary:

We know the name JESUS is a supernatural name because God gave Jesus his name. The name JESUS was also given to Joseph, in a dream. **Matthew 1:21**.God tells us that Salvation, healing, protection, prosperity, eternal life is to found only in the name of Jesus. **Acts 4:12**. How powerful is that name? All power in heaven and in earth has been given to Jesus. **Matthew 28:18**. Every knee in heaven, in the earth and under the earth must bow to the name of Jesus. **Philippians 2:10.** So, be 100% confident in the name of Jesus and use that name in everything, every day of your life, fully conscious of its supernatural origin and unlimited power. So when you confront evil supernatural powers, be 100% confident in the name of Jesus. Demonic powers know Jesus and they will know you too and must flee from you. **Acts 19:15. James 4:7**. We know God cannot lie. **Titus 1:2.**

Prayer: Father, I forgive everyone who has offended me and pray you to forgive my sins. In Jesus name, I destroy every satanic power, strategy and plot against my life, my finances and health. Lord God, give me boldness to speak to everyone about you. Give me strength to overcome all difficulties and achieve all my goals and objectives in life. Help me make wise decisions today. Lord, give me my daily bread. Lead and Guide me. Bless me and bless all the works of my hand. Father, keep me safe from all evil and temptations in Jesus name.

Confession & Meditation: The name of Jesus is supernatural and powerful.

Questions and Notes for further study:

1. What is God saying to you through this devotion and meditation?

2. What will you put into practice in your life?

Your Review after 4 weeks:

3. How has it affected your life?

4. What more could you do?

DAY 34

Scripture KJV: Jeremiah 29:11

"... For I know the thoughts (plans) that I think towards (have for) you, says the LORD, thoughts (plans) of peace, and not of evil, to give you an expected end..."

Commentary:

God says He knows the thoughts and plans He has for you this 2015 and for the rest of the years of your life. What are these thoughts and plans? Plans of peace to give you an expected end. What is an expected end? Remember **Matthew 7:10** and **Luke 11:11**? Will any father give a stone to his child who asks for bread or give a snake to his child who asks him for a fish? The child expects a bread and fish not a stone or a snake. Remember the feeding of the five thousand – what did Jesus feed them with? Bread and Fish. **Matthew 15:36** so, the expected end God is talking about in **Jeremiah 29:11** is the answer to your prayers. We know this because God says so in **Jeremiah 29:12**, when He says you shall call on him, and pray to him, and He *will* listen to you because He loves you with an Everlasting Love. **Jeremiah 31:3** God cannot lie. **Titus 1:2.**

Prayer: Father, I forgive everyone who has offended me and pray you to forgive my sins. Lord, thank you for your plans, thoughts and your everlasting love for me. Lord,

I love you forever. Father, give me boldness to speak to everyone about you. Give me strength to overcome all difficulties and achieve all your goals and objectives for my life. Help me make wise decisions. Lord, give me my daily bread. Lead and Guide me. Bless me and bless all the works of my hand and keep me safe from all evil and temptations in Jesus name.

Confession & Meditation: God has plans for me and they are good plans.

Questions and Notes for further study:

1. What is God saying to you through this devotion and meditation?

2. What will you put into practice in your life?

Your Review after 4 weeks:

3. How has it affected your life?

4. What more could you do?

DAY 35

Scripture KJV: Romans 1:16
"... For I am not ashamed of the gospel of Christ: for it is the power of God to salvation to everyone that believes; to the Jew first, and also to the Greek..."

Commentary:

Everyone seeks the Power of God. Where is the Power of God? God tells us that his power is in the Gospel of Christ and is available ONLY to those who BELIEVES. Salvation means a lot of different things like deliverance, healing, prosperity etc. Most people belief limit the Power of God only to the part of salvation that they believe in. How do you know if you believe? Look at the Story of Peter walking on water. **Matthew 14:28-32**. Peter believed and walked on water. Peter took his eyes off Jesus and began to look at the circumstances, storms and doubt the truth of the word of Jesus. He began to sink. God tells us that Jesus is the Truth. **John 14:6**. Jesus is the Power of God. **1 Corinthians 1:24**. You shall know the truth and the Truth has the power to make you free. **John 8:32.** God cannot lie. **Titus 1:2**

Prayer: Father, I forgive everyone who has offended me and pray you to forgive my sins. Lord, thank you for your plans, thoughts and your everlasting love for me. Lord,

I love you forever. Father, give me boldness to speak to everyone about you. Give me strength to overcome all difficulties and achieve all your goals and objectives for my life. Help me make wise decisions. Lord, give me my daily bread. Lead and Guide me. Bless me and bless all the works of my hand and keep me safe from all evil and temptations in Jesus name.

Confession & Meditation: The Gospel is the power of God for my salvation.

Questions and Notes for further study:

1. What is God saying to you through this devotion and meditation?

2. What will you put into practice in your life?

Your Review after 4 weeks:

3. How has it affected your life?

4. What more could you do?

DAY 36

Scripture KJV: Jeremiah 30:17
"... For I will restore health to you, and I will heal you of your wounds, said the LORD; because they called you an Outcast, saying, this is Zion, whom no man seeks after..."

Commentary:
All sickness are curses for anyone who broke God's laws. **Deuteronomy 28:15 – 68.** God is the healer. **Exodus 15:26. Psalm 103:33.** Medical science derive their knowledge from him. How does God heal? He sends his WORD. **Psalm 107:20**. Note that the bible says his WORD not his Words. Who is this WORD? He is JESUS. John 1:1 tells us that the Word was God. **John 1:14,** tells us that the Word was made flesh, and dwelled among us. How did he dwell amongst us? **Luke 1:35 – 37** tells us that Jesus was born of the word of God. How did he become our healer? By taking our sins on his own body and healing us by his wounds. **1Peter 2:24.** How exactly did this happen? **Galatians 1:13** tells us that he did it by taking our place by becoming a curse for us i.e. suffering that disease or sickness so we never have to suffer it. God cannot lie. **Titus 1:2**

Prayer: Father, I forgive everyone who has offended me and pray you to forgive my sins. Lord, thank you for your plans, thoughts and your everlasting love for me. Lord, I love you forever. Father, give me boldness to speak to everyone about you. Give me strength to overcome all difficulties and achieve all your goals and objectives for my life. Help me make wise decisions. Lord, give me my daily bread. Lead and Guide me. Bless me and bless all the works of my hand and keep me safe from all evil and temptations in Jesus name.

Confession & Meditation: God restores health and healing to me.

Questions and Notes for further study:

1. What is God saying to you through this devotion and meditation?

2. What will you put into practice in your life?

Your Review after 4 weeks:

3. How has it affected your life?

4. What more could you do?

DAY 37

Scripture KJV: 2 Timothy 1:7
"... For God has not given us the spirit of fear; but of power, and of love, and of a sound mind..."

Commentary:
God has given us the Spirit of Sound Mind. This is the mind of God, the mind of Christ. **1 Corinthians 2:16**. Webster's 1828 English Dictionary says that the Mind means many different things in different contexts. It can mean your will; memory; your understanding; your opinions; your emotions. The mind is invisible and so very important as it is the gateway into your spirit and is part of your spirit. You keep your mind when you die. That is why you are renew it with the word of God. **Romans 12:2.** God promises to keep you in perfect peace only if your mind is stayed on him, because you trust him. **Isaiah 26:3.** How do you do this? By keeping the word of God in your mind day and night. **Proverbs 3:21; Joshua 1:8; Psalm 1:2.** If you do this faithfully everyday of your life, you will enjoy **Psalm 1:3** everyday of your life. God cannot lie. **Titus 1:2**

Prayer: Father, I forgive everyone who has offended me and pray you to forgive my sins. Lord, thank you for your plans, thoughts and your everlasting love for me. Lord, I love you forever. Father, give me boldness to speak to everyone about you. Give me strength to overcome all difficulties and achieve all your goals and objectives for my life. Help me make wise decisions. Lord, give me my daily bread. Lead and Guide me. Bless me and bless all the works of my hand and keep me safe from all evil and temptations in Jesus name.

Confession & Meditation: God has not given me the spirit of fear.

Questions and Notes for further study:

1. What is God saying to you through this devotion and meditation?

2. What will you put into practice in your life?

Your Review after 4 weeks:

3. How has it affected your life?

4. What more could you do?

DAY 38

Scripture KJV: 2 Timothy 1:7
"... For God has not given us the spirit of fear..."

Commentary:

God has not given us the Spirit of Fear. What is fear? It is a spirit that manifests itself as an emotion that is caused by an expectation of evil or hurt. It has torment. **1John 4:18.** It can be of three kinds. Fear of man and or people. Fear of Satan. Fear of God. God calls the fear of man or people a trap. Proverbs 29:25. We are not to fear people. The fear of Satan brings bondage to death. **Hebrews 2:14-15.** We are not to fear Satan. The fear of the Lord is the only fear we are to have. **Psalm 34:9. Matthew 10:28. Luke 12:5.** It brings life, protection and peace. What is the fear of the Lord? It is to hate evil, pride, evil way, lying and keep all God's commandments. **Proverbs 8:13. Ecclesiastes 12:13**. God desires we serve him without fear of man or Satan. **Luke 1:74**. What should you do when you are tempted to fear man or Satan? Resist that fear continuously in the name of Jesus until it flees from you. **James 4:7.**God cannot lie. **Titus 1:2**

Prayer: Father, I forgive everyone who has offended me and pray you to forgive my sins. Lord, thank you for giving me the spirit of power, love and sound mind. Lord, I love you forever. Father, give me boldness to speak to everyone about you. Give me strength to overcome all difficulties and achieve all your goals and objectives for my life. Help me make wise decisions. Lord, give me my daily bread. Lead and Guide me. Bless me and bless all the works of my hand and keep me safe from all evil and temptations in Jesus name.

Confession & Meditation: God has given me the Spirit of Power; Love and of Sound mind.

Questions and Notes for further study:

1. What is God saying to you through this devotion and meditation?

2. What will you put into practice in your life?

Your Review after 4 weeks:

3. How has it affected your life?

4. What more could you do?

DAY 39

Scripture KJV: Psalm 5:11
"...But let all those that put their trust in you rejoice: let them ever shout for joy, because you defend them: let them also that love your name be joyful in you..."

Commentary:

Is your trust in God? If not, why not? If yes, then you should rejoice and shout for joy. Why should you shout for joy? You shout for joy because God is your defender and there is fullness of Joy in his presence. **Psalm 16:11** and if God be for you, who can be against you? **Romans 8:31.** One side of God is that He is a joyful God who rejoices over you with joy and singing. **John 15:11. Zephaniah 3:17.** His Joy is our strength. **Nehemiah 8:10.** We are told in **Ephesians 6:10** to be strong in the Lord and in his mighty power. One aspect of being strong in God is to be strong in Joy for Joy is a fruit of the Spirit. **Galatians 5:22.** How do you get joyful? By counting your blessings one by one; being grateful to God for sending Jesus to save us; speaking to people about Jesus and counting all trials and tests as all joy. **James 1:2.** God cannot lie. **Titus 1:2**

Prayer: Father, I forgive everyone who has offended me and ask you to forgive my sins. I rejoice and thank you for the multitude of blessings you have blessed me with in Jesus name. Father, bless and prosper me. Give me boldness to speak to everyone about you. Give me strength to overcome all difficulties and achieve all goals and objectives in life. Help me make wise decisions; give me my daily bread and lead and guide me and keep me safe from all evil and temptations in Jesus name.

Confession & Meditation: I shout for joy for God is my joy and delight forever.

Questions and Notes for further study:

1. What is God saying to you through this devotion and meditation?

2. What will you put into practice in your life?

Your Review after 4 weeks:

3. How has it affected your life?

4. What more could you do?

DAY 40

Scripture KJV: John 14:1

"... Let not your heart be troubled: you believe in God, believe also in me. ..."

Commentary:

Your heart is your spirit and the most important part of you. God calls the heart, the hidden man of the heart. **1 Peter 3:4.** Out of your heart all the issues of life flow. **Proverbs 4:23.** The heart is deceitful above all things, and desperately wicked: who can know it? **Jeremiah 17:9. Matthew 15:19.** But we have a new heart and spirit. **Ezekiel 36:26. Hebrews 8:10**. We can now do all things through Christ's strength. **Philippians 4:13.** We have the power to not let our heart be afraid or troubled no matter what comes our way. How? By being a doer of God's word. **James 1:25.** By loving God, with all our heart, soul, understanding, strength, and loving our neighbor as yourself. **Mark 12:33.** Jesus gave us his Peace. The peace that passes all understanding. **John 14:27. Philippians 4:7.** Do you have any trouble? Pour out all your heart before God and then wait on the LORD. **Psalm 62:8. Psalm 27:14**. He will rescue you. God cannot lie. **Titus 1:2**

Prayer: Father, I forgive everyone who has offended me and ask you to forgive my sins. I pour out all my heart before you and wait on you Lord. Lord, deliver me out of all my troubles. Father, bless and prosper me. Lord, give me my daily bread. Lead and Guide me. Bless me and bless all the works of my hand. Father, keep me safe from all evil and temptations in Jesus name.

Confession & Meditation: I will not let my heart be troubled for God is with me and will deliver me from every trouble.

Questions and Notes for further study:

1. What is God saying to you through this devotion and meditation?

2. What will you put into practice in your life?

FEED YOUR SPIRIT

Your Review after 4 weeks:

3. How has it affected your life?

4. What more could you do?